MODERN ROLE MODELS

Tony Parker

Chuck Bednar

Mason Crest Publishers

Produced by OTTN Publishing in association with
21st Century Publishing and Communications, Inc.

MASON CREST PUBLISHERS INC.
370 Reed Road
Broomall, Pennsylvania 19008
(866) MCP-BOOK (toll free)
www.masoncrest.com

Printed in the United States of America.

First Printing

9 8 7 6 5 4 3 2 1

Library of Congress Cataloging-in-Publication Data

Bednar, Chuck, 1976–
    Tony Parker / Chuck Bednar.
       p. cm. — (Modern role models)
    ISBN 978-1-4222-0486-3 (hardcover) — ISBN 978-1-4222-0774-1 (pbk.)
    1. Parker, William Anthony, 1982–   —Juvenile literature. 2. Basketball players—United States—Biography—Juvenile literature. I. Title.
    GV884.P37B436 2009
    796.323092—dc22
    [B]   2008025064

Publisher's note:
All quotations in this book come from original sources, and contain the spelling and grammatical inconsistencies of the original text.

CROSS-CURRENTS

*In the ebb and flow of the currents of life we are each influenced by many people, places, and events that we directly experience or have learned about. Throughout the chapters of this book you will come across **CROSS-CURRENTS** reference boxes. These boxes direct you to a **CROSS-CURRENTS** section in the back of the book that contains fascinating and informative sidebars and related pictures. Go on. ▶▶*

CONTENTS

Savoring the moment, San Antonio Spurs guard Tony Parker holds the NBA Championship trophy in his right hand and the NBA Finals MVP trophy in his left hand, June 14, 2007. Tony's outstanding play had made him the first European-born player to be honored as the Finals MVP, and it had helped the Spurs sweep the Cleveland Cavaliers to win their fourth NBA title.

1

Champion and MVP

TONY PARKER HAD BEEN MANY THINGS EARLY ON in his National Basketball Association (NBA) career. He had been a **rookie** sensation, an All-Star player, and a playoff contender. He had even been a world champion—twice. He had also attracted media attention off the **court** because of the celebrity company he kept.

Life had been pretty good to Tony Parker. But, in June 2007, Tony was about to rise to a new level of fame and professional success. Tony and his team, the San Antonio Spurs, were playing LeBron James and the Cleveland Cavaliers in the NBA Finals. The Spurs had entered the series as the old guard, a team of experienced veterans who had been down this road before. The Cavaliers, and particularly James, their star player, were the new blood and the future of the league. Many thought their time had come, but Tony Parker and his teammates had different plans, and they wasted little time **executing** them.

In Game 1 of the NBA Finals, Tony Parker scored 27 points and added seven **assists** in an 85–76 victory. In Game 2, he scored

30 points as San Antonio beat Cleveland, 103–92. And in the third game of the series, the San Antonio **point guard** scored 17 points in yet another Spurs victory.

ON THE THRESHOLD OF GREATNESS

Hot on the heels of those first three games, the whispers began. Tony had averaged 25 points per game to that point in the 2007 NBA Finals. He was averaging just under five assists per game, too, as he emerged from the supporting role that he had held during past championship runs. He was turning into one of the team's leading men.

CROSS-CURRENTS

To learn more about the history of Tony Parker's team, check out "The San Antonio Spurs." Go to page 47. ▶▶

Tony Parker wasn't the only Spurs star leading the charge against the Cavaliers, though. Tim Duncan, Manu Ginobili, and Bruce Bowen, among others, also deserved credit for the team's success. Still, the whispers persisted. Tony Parker should be named the 2007 NBA Finals **MVP**. If he was, he would be the first European-born player in the history of the game to earn the honor. Tony was humbled by the very thought of it. As he told NBA.com's Martin C. Sumners prior to Game 4:

> **"That would be unbelievable. But I still think Timmy [Duncan] is going to get it because he's our franchise and he's a superstar. But if they want to change, why not? But still—I'm joking. But still, there's one more game, and if we win the championship, I'll be very happy with that. . . . I'd be the first one to be very happy."**

With those thoughts in the back of his mind, and the whispers of his MVP-like performance persisting right up until game time, Tony Parker led the Spurs out onto the court for Game 4 of the 2007 NBA Finals on June 14. Cleveland jumped out to a 20–19 lead in the first quarter and played tough all night long. Having trailed by as many as 11 points, the Cavs staged a rally in the third and fourth quarters, rattling off 14 straight points to take their first second-half lead in the Finals. The Spurs put together a dramatic 12–3 rally as well, however, and prevailed in an 83–82 nail-biter to claim their fourth

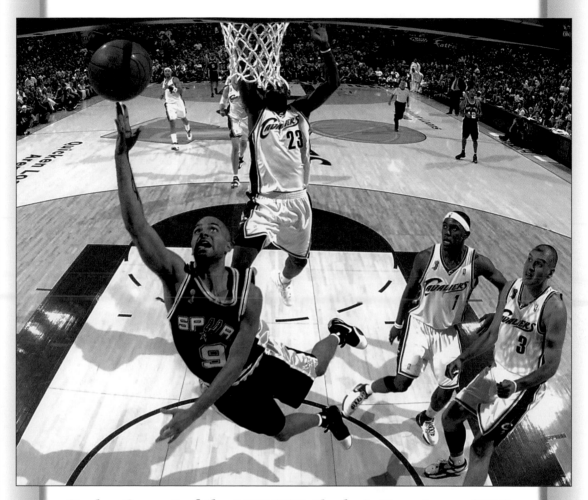

During Game 4 of the 2007 NBA Finals, LeBron James (#23) makes a futile attempt to block a Tony Parker layup from behind as his Cleveland Cavaliers teammates Daniel Gibson (#1) and Aleksandar Pavlovic (#3) watch helplessly. Tony scored 24 points on 10-for-14 shooting to eliminate the Cavs and seal the title for San Antonio.

NBA Championship in nine seasons. Tony scored 24 points and added 7 **rebounds** on the evening.

Once the final buzzer sounded and the title was officially secure, all eyes turned toward the MVP award presentation. People were eager to see whether Tony Parker would bring home the hardware and make professional basketball history.

⇒ MOST VALUABLE, INDEED ⇐

The whispers were right: Tony Parker was named the Most Valuable Player for his performance in the NBA Finals, which included leading the team with a 24.5 points per game scoring average and a 56.8 **shooting percentage**. Clearly, he deserved the award. Tony was overwhelmed—not just because of what being MVP meant for himself or for his team, but also because he was the first European-born player to win the trophy. As the new MVP said in a July 15 interview with InsideHoops.com:

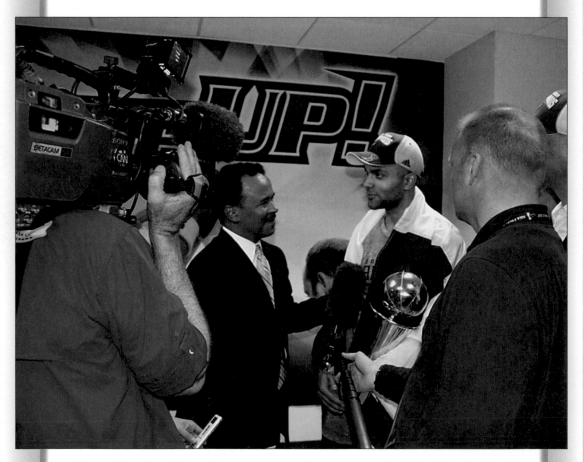

After the decisive Game 4, newly crowned NBA Finals MVP Tony Parker is interviewed by CNN sports reporter Larry Smith, June 14, 2007. In just his sixth season in the NBA, the 25-year-old star, who was raised in France, had already won his third championship ring.

> **"It's great, it's great. It's just unbelievable. I'm speechless. When I look at that trophy, I'm going to wake up tomorrow and it's still going to be a dream. European basketball is improving every year. You've got Dirk Nowitzki [of Germany] the MVP for the first time [in 2007] and now [me for] the MVP Finals. There's going to be more."**

The NBA Finals MVP was not the only honor that was bestowed upon Tony in 2007. He also won the European Player of the Year award for the year 2007, beating out many other talented athletes, including Dirk Nowitzki, the Dallas Mavericks' star who had been selected as the NBA's Most Valuable Player in 2007. Nowitzki had won the European Player of the Year award in each of the previous five years.

The 2006–07 season had been a banner one for Tony. In addition to his average of 18.6 points and 5.5 assists, he pulled down 3.2 rebounds per game during the regular season. It was the pinnacle of his young career to that point, a career that had seen a teenage basketball player arrive from France, make an immediate impact on the game, survive some turbulence along the way, and establish himself as a role model, pop-culture icon, and sports star on the rise.

CROSS-CURRENTS

Read "European Player of the Year Award" to find out more about NBA players who have won this honor over the years. Go to page 47. ▶▶

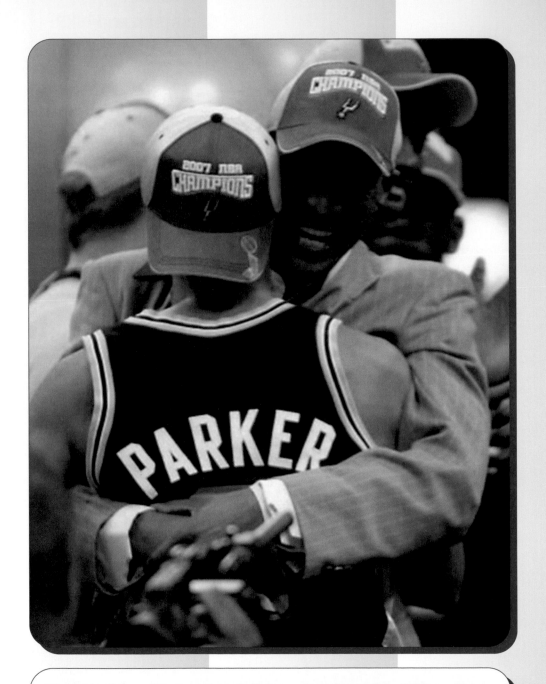

Tony Parker gets a congratulatory hug from his father, Tony Parker Sr., following the Spurs 2007 NBA Championship victory. The elder Tony Parker had himself been an elite basketball player. After starring at Loyola University in Chicago, he played for 15 years in European pro leagues.

Basketball in His Blood

WILLIAM ANTHONY PARKER JR. WAS BORN ON
May 17, 1982. His father, Tony Parker Sr., was an American-born professional basketball player, and his mother, Pamela Firestone, was a Dutch fashion model. Tony is the oldest of three children in his family and has two younger brothers, Terrence (T.J.) and Pierre.

Tony was born in Bruges, Belgium. He spent most of his childhood and young adult life in Paris, however, so most people identify him with France.

Tony and his brothers inherited their father's love of basketball and his aptitude for the game. The elder Tony Parker was a star with Loyola University in Chicago, and Tony Jr. has often said that his father could have starred with the NBA Chicago Bulls had he not chosen to

CROSS-CURRENTS

To learn more about the country that Tony Parker calls home, check out "Facts About France." Go to page 48. ▶▶

11

play in Europe. Even so, Tony Sr. put together quite a résumé as a ballplayer, playing 15 seasons, winning titles in Belgium and the Netherlands, and winning the French National Championship in 1984.

The Parker family was on the move during Tony's childhood, accompanying Tony Sr. around Europe with his various teams. In the summers, they visited Chicago to see their grandparents. Tony and his brothers worked on their English and on their basketball and soccer, playing in the city where their father had grown up.

➤ FROM SOCCER TO THE COURTS ➤

Tony Parker was a talented athlete even as a child, and his first game was soccer. Playing center fullback, Tony scored many goals and enjoyed the game immensely. He was also a big fan of Michael Jordan and the Chicago Bulls, however. When Tony met Jordan in Chicago, he knew immediately that soccer was in his past. From that point on, his future was clear. He would be a basketball player, like MJ and like his father, his two role models.

Tony chose the point guard position and began his pro career in France at the age of 15. In 1997, after one year of play, he was named MVP of the Salbris Junior Tournament. There he was discovered by INSEP, the French National Institute of Sports and Physical Education. Founded in 1947, INSEP provides gifted young athletes the chance to study and live together while they train for a career in sports under internationally experienced teachers, trainers, and medical experts. Many of France's Olympic athletes train and study at INSEP, and it is a model for other countries. Tony was invited to attend the Paris-based institute, where he studied basketball while playing against athletes ranging in age from 17 to 38.

➤ GROWING AS A PLAYER ➤

After graduating from INSEP and earning the equivalent of a high school diploma, Tony played for the French Junior National Team in the 1998 European Junior Championship and the following year signed with Paris Saint-Germain (PS-G). Although he was only a reserve player with PS-G, Tony had the opportunity to study and learn from one of the best. On his official Web site, he shared the experience:

"It is not easy to become famous playing back-up to a point guard like Laurent Sciarra. He plays

almost all the time, and even just had one of his best seasons. . . . [but] I learned so much about the professional world of basketball by watching how one directs the team. **"**

Tony used the knowledge and experience he had picked up from playing with Sciarra, as well as from his father and INSEP, to make an outstanding showing at the 2000 Nike Hoop Summit, an event pitting the best players from the United States against the best from the rest of the world in an exhibition game. In front of an audience of college coaches, recruiters, and NBA scouts, Tony was impressive.

Tony Parker, playing for the French Junior National Team, dribbles the ball during action from the European Junior Championships, 2000. Tony, who began his professional career at the tender age of 15, gained basketball experience at the French National Institute of Sports and Physical Education and on the Paris Saint-Germain team.

He scored 20 points and had seven assists on the day, catching the eye of more than one talent judge.

Afterwards, he returned to France for what would be his farewell tour in Europe. Tony joined the French Junior National squad and led them to the European Junior League Championship. He averaged 25.8 points and 6.8 assists during the tournament and was named Junior League MVP. He also played in 30 games for Paris Basket Racing that season, averaging almost 15 points per game.

⇛ THE NBA COMES CALLING ⇚

Tony's stock continued to rise as he demonstrated what he was capable of on a basketball court. Several U.S. universities, including longtime NCAA powerhouse UCLA and Georgia Tech, came calling for his services. Tony, however, was not interested in going to college:

> **"For all basketball players, the real dream is to play in the NBA. It is in the NBA that the best players play. In France, if you talk to little boys, they know all of the NBA players and not one single Pro A player. And, even though, it is not the most important thing, you have to realize that in the NBA the lowest paid player still makes more than the highest paid player in France."**

So Tony made his decision. He would leave France and Paris Basket Racing, but would not go to college. Instead, he decided to take a gamble. He would declare himself eligible for the 2001 National Basketball Association **draft** and see if there were any takers.

As it turned out, one man who had his eyes on Tony Parker at the Nike Hoop Summit was R.C. Buford, the assistant general manager of the San Antonio Spurs. As Buford told *USA Today*'s David DuPree:

CROSS-CURRENTS

Read "Other European NBA Players" to learn about some basketball stars who left Europe for the NBA. Go to page 50. ▶▶

> **"He was playing out of position . . . and the other team had . . . a bunch of big-time American players. Tony just kicked their behinds and acted like it was no big deal. . . . I just thought Tony had a maturity**

about him, and I liked the fact that he had been in a pro locker room since he was 16 and knew how to deal with a mature locker room like we had. **"**

Buford had to work hard to convince Spurs coach Gregg Popovich. The coach was not impressed with Tony's size. At 6 feet 2 inches tall, Tony is not big in a sport where many players top out at more than 7 feet. Buford had a front office intern compile a video-tape of Parker highlights and sat down with Popovich to review the tape. The coach had a complete change of heart, even telling Buford that he thought Tony would be a starter before the end of his rookie season. Having won over his coach, Buford got his guy. On June 27, 2001, San Antonio selected Tony Parker with the 28th pick in the first round. Tony was officially headed to the NBA.

➤ TONY'S NBA DEBUT ◄

As it happened, Popovich's prediction came true. After working hard in the NBA's summer league and in Spurs training camp, 19-year-old Tony worked his way into the starting lineup after just five regular-season games. He was the first rookie to be named a starter during the 2001–02 season, and he made an immediate impact, recording 12 points, four assists, and three rebounds during a November game against the Orlando Magic.

Any questions about Tony's basketball abilities had been answered, and he continued to play well the whole regular season. As a rookie, he played in 77 games, becoming the first European point guard ever to play in the NBA and the youngest player in San Antonio Spurs history. He averaged 9.2 points, 4.3 assists, 2.6 rebounds, and 1.2 **steals** per game. He led his team in assists in 35 of his 77 games and in steals 27 times. In the end, he was the Spurs season leader in those two categories and was named to the NBA All-Rookie First Team, the first foreign-born guard to bring home such an honor. He was just a rookie, but even at such a young age, it was clear that Tony Parker was something special.

In the early months of his second NBA season, 2002–03, Tony Parker played inconsistently. However, as the season progressed, he took on an increasingly important role for the Spurs. His minutes per game rose, and Tony improved his shooting accuracy. At 15.5 points per game, Tony's 2002–03 scoring average was up more than 6 points from his rookie season.

3

Highs and Lows

TONY'S ROOKIE SEASON HAD BEEN A SUCCESS IN many ways, but the road to NBA success had not been without its bumps. He played alongside some of the best players in the game, including David Robinson and Tim Duncan. Those two star players, as well as Coach Popovich, continually challenged Tony to become a better player.

Although he had become a starter almost instantly, his coach and his teammates still considered Tony to be a work in progress. As he recalled in an interview with Dan Wetzel of Yahoo! Sports:

CROSS-CURRENTS

To learn about the life and career of Tony's coach with the Spurs, read "The Man Called Pop." Go to page 51. ▶▶

❝There [were] growing pains for me. You know, Coach Pop was really, really hard on me, always trying to push me and looking for perfection. I thought I was doing pretty good. But it was never enough.

> **I could score 14, 15; it was never enough. Sometimes I felt like it wasn't fair, all the criticism.** 🙶

Tony kept working, though, and he was becoming an even better player. In the playoffs following the 2001–02 season, Tony played in 10 games and averaged 15.5 points, 4.0 assists, and 2.9 rebounds. In his biggest game of the postseason that year, Tony scored 24 points and dished 5 assists against the Los Angeles Lakers in the third game of the Western Conference Finals. Parker, Duncan, Robinson, and company lost four straight games to the Lakers, however, and were eliminated from the NBA Playoffs. It was a sign of things to come in the career of Tony Parker—there would be peaks, and there would be valleys.

⟫ SOPHOMORE SENSATION OR SOPHOMORE SLUMP? ⟪

Tony felt both highs and lows right from the beginning during his second season in the NBA. In the Spurs' first game of that 2002–03 season, he missed all 10 shots he took, although San Antonio did manage to defeat Los Angeles. At his peak, in December, he put together the highest-scoring game of his young career, 32 points in a December 11 game against the Dallas Mavericks. (His previous high had been 22 points.) He then duplicated the feat later that month against the Chicago Bulls.

Following the Dallas game—a seesaw battle in which the Spurs led by 10 points, trailed by 16, led by 19, and saw that lead dwindle to 5 before they finally sealed the win, 111–104—Tony told Johnny Ludden of the *San Antonio Express-News*:

> 🙶**I never lost my confidence. As a basketball player, you can never do that. . . . Even if you're shooting bad, the point guard is still the head of the snake. You have to bring something.** 🙶

Tony continued to be an inconsistent shooter for the first several months of the 2002–03 campaign. One night he would connect on 60 percent of his shots, and two games later he would score on just one-third of his attempts. In 8 of his first 19 games, Tony connected on fewer than 40 percent of his shots, and five times during that span he posted less than 10 points in a game. Only once,

With the Portland Trail Blazers' 6'11" forward Rasheed Wallace playing tenacious defense under the basket, Tony Parker dishes a pass to a Spurs teammate. As San Antonio's point guard, Tony carried the primary responsibility for running the team's offense. But early in his career, his passing wasn't overly impressive: Tony ranked just 22nd in the NBA in assists per game in 2002–03.

on November 11, could he manage a double-digit assist figure, and only four times did he have at least eight.

The trend continued for much of December as well, with Tony's shooting percentage rising as high as .667 and dipping as low .167 during the month. One night he only made a pair of assists, and the very next game, he dished out 10 of them. Flashes of brilliance were followed by nights of mediocrity. Tony wasn't having a bad season by anyone's measure, but he was starting to be fitted with the dreaded label of inconsistency. Tony, his teammates, and his coach all realized the same thing—something had to change.

➤ NEW YEAR, NEW TONY ➤

And change it did! Tony worked hard to improve his shooting, and as 2002 gave way to 2003, the work began to pay off. Tony still had off nights, but they were getting fewer and farther between. He shot 50 percent or better in 7 of the 14 games the Spurs played in January, twice topping 72 percent. Then, in February, he ran off a string of seven 50 percent or better shooting performances in an eight-game span, including four-straight 20-point performances.

It was no coincidence that, as Tony's level of play began to stabilize, the Spurs began to enjoy success as a team. During the months of January and February, San Antonio lost only four games and won eight games in a row. On March 1, they beat the Sacramento Kings, 108–100, for their 40th victory of the season. Tony led the way in that contest, scoring 19 first-quarter points en route to a 32-point, five-assist day. Still, the Spurs found themselves trailing the Dallas Mavericks in the Midwest Division. On March 21, San Antonio beat Dallas, 112–110 in overtime, to pull within two and a half games of the Mavericks. And who was it that hit the game winner? None other than Tony Parker.

Closer and closer they crept to the division title, eventually taking the lead over the Mavericks, who at one point had led the Midwest by more than eight games. When, on April 14, the Spurs defeated the Utah Jazz, 91–83, they had the best record in the NBA. Tony Parker came up big in the game, scoring 9 of his 25 points in the last four minutes to secure the victory. The Spurs finished the 2002–03 regular season with a 60–22 record, and they entered the 2003 playoffs as the number-one seed in the Western Conference. Tony ended the regular season averaging 15.5 points, 5.3 assists,

An inspired stretch drive enabled San Antonio to finish the 2002–03 regular season with a 60–22 record—and home-court advantage throughout the Western Conference playoffs. Although Tony Parker's fine play had been key to the Spurs' success, the postseason brought the young point guard more than his share of frustrations.

and 2.6 rebounds while playing in all 82 games. Despite his early inconsistency, he had emerged as a key component in the Spurs' offense, with the team winning an amazing 20 out of the 21 games in which Tony scored at least 20 points.

Juwon Howard (#5) of the Dallas Mavericks tries to prevent a soaring Tony Parker from finding an open teammate as Mavs guard Steve Nash (left) and Spurs center David Robinson (right) look on. Tony started the 2003 Western Conference Finals strong, averaging 22.7 points in the first four games. But then he virtually disappeared, scoring just 7 points in Game 5 and getting blanked in Game 6.

➤ A Whole New Ballgame ➤

Despite Tony's success during the regular season, he had learned as a rookie that the playoffs presented different challenges. At first, it didn't look as if he would be up to those challenges. In the first game of San Antonio's opening-round series against the Phoenix Suns, he managed only seven points on 2-of-13 shooting from the floor and was 0-for-6 from **three-point** range. He struggled defensively against Suns guard Stephon Marbury as well. Tony's hard times continued into Game 2, and the young point guard was replaced by Speedy Claxton in the lineup.

Tony came back strong in Game 3, scoring 29 points in a San Antonio victory, but the inconsistency that had plagued him early in his second season of regular play was a problem once again in the postseason. He scored 19 points in a Game 4 loss, but only 4 of those points came in the second half. In San Antonio's Game 5 victory, he managed just 7 points, but then he scored 17 in Game 6, which was also a San Antonio win. His streaky play continued even as the Spurs went on to eliminate both the Los Angeles Lakers and the Dallas Mavericks on their way to the NBA Finals. He would play amazing basketball one night, and the next he would play poorly enough to force Coach Popovich to use Claxton or Steve Kerr in his place. However inconsistent his performance may have become on the court, this much was crystal clear: Soon Tony Parker and his teammates would be playing on the NBA's biggest stage, with the biggest prize in professional basketball at stake.

➤ More Than a Title at Stake ➤

Playing for an NBA Championship should have been the most exciting moment in Tony's young career, and in many ways it was. But the thrill was tempered by rumors that the man he would face off against, Jason Kidd of the Eastern Conference champion New Jersey Nets, was headed to San Antonio the following season to replace him as the Spurs' starting point guard. There was a feeling in the air that Tony was not only playing to help his team win the title— he might very well be playing to keep his job. Tony really felt the pressure as the series began.

Tony responded well to the pressure in Game 1, scoring 16 points as San Antonio beat New Jersey 101–89. Kidd, meanwhile, finished with only 10 points on 4-of-11 shooting from the floor. Kidd

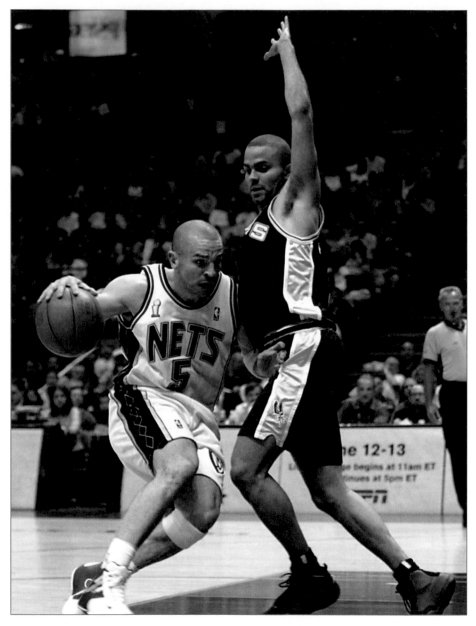

Tony Parker defends Jason Kidd in action from Game 3 of the NBA Finals, June 8, 2003. Throughout the series, the matchup between the New Jersey and San Antonio point guards provided drama. Tony got the better of Kidd in Game 3, scoring 26 points to pace the Spurs to an 84–79 victory. Kidd, meanwhile, scored just 12.

and the Nets took round two, though, with the New Jersey point guard scoring 30 points compared to Tony Parker's 21 and leading his team to an 87–85 victory. Headed into Game 3, the game-within-the-game between the two guards continued to be one of the biggest stories of the series. It was a lot for a young player like Tony to handle, but as Ludden observed, he didn't let the chatter get to him:

> **Parker knew he would have to deal with the 2,137 Jason Kidd questions in these NBA Finals. He knew he would have to listen to the hang-up-and-listen experts debate whether the Spurs should pursue Kidd this summer to play alongside him, replace him or spend their free-agent dollars elsewhere. . . . Each time he was asked, Parker gave the same answer. He shrugged. He couldn't control what the Spurs did in the future, he said. All he could do was play.**

His demeanor and focus were commendable, especially for a second-year athlete, and in Game 3, Tony scored 26 points and led a Spurs comeback that resulted in an 84–79 San Antonio victory. But he couldn't maintain the momentum in Game 4, missing 11 of 12 shots from the field. After a much-needed talking to from his coach during the fifth game, he finished with 14 points. But he mustered just four points and two assists in Game 6. Nevertheless, the Spurs won the game, 88–77, to seal the NBA Championship.

Once it was all said and done, Tony Parker was among those celebrating the title in the locker room. But questions about his future as the point guard of the San Antonio Spurs remained unanswered as he moved into the off-season.

Tony Parker lays one in during a game against the Memphis Grizzlies at San Antonio's SBC Center, December 15, 2003. San Antonio won the game, 78–67. Despite persistent rumors that the Spurs were planning to replace Tony during the 2003–04 season, the team stuck with its third-year point guard. He responded with more consistent play.

Rising Above

IN HIS HOME COUNTRY OF FRANCE, TONY PARKER was a big star. During his first two seasons with the Spurs, the young point guard had become a national treasure to sports fans in his homeland. French spectators began showing up at Spurs games, waving signs written in French to show their support for Tony.

CROSS-CURRENTS

To learn about other sports stars from around the world, read "International Sports Stars." Go to page 52. ▶▶

That popularity increased as his team made its way through the playoffs and won the 2003 NBA Championship. Television ratings for NBA games were up in France and all across Europe, as the Tony Parker phenomenon spread like wildfire. Tom Marchesi of NBA Europe later told ESPN.com:

❝Since his first championship with the Spurs in 2003, things have really taken off. That year he was named Sportsman of the Year by *L'Equipe*, which is the most widely read newspaper in France. When you consider the list of people who have won that award, that was an incredible achievement for a basketball player. From there, his popularity and people's awareness of him went up in leaps and bounds. **"**

⟫ A COMMITMENT TO EXCELLENCE ⟪

The story was a little different in the United States, though. Despite being the starting point guard for the newly crowned NBA Champions, young Tony Parker still didn't have a clear view of his future. His erratic performance in the Finals only fanned the rumors that he was going to be replaced by Jason Kidd. Buzz had it that, once Kidd was brought in, Parker would be asked to switch to shooting guard. The prospect of being replaced did not sit well with Tony, as he later told Dan Wetzel:

> **"**[It] was a tough time for me because I was 21 and we just won a championship and they wanted Jason Kidd. It's hard to accept. I told [Coach Popovich], 'I want to be the point guard. I want to do it and I'm going to work hard to become a great player.' . . . You know, it worked out for the best even if it was harder. I was happy to go through that because it made me a better player. With Pop, it was like a father-and-son relationship. And even sometimes, you know, I thought he was crazy, but it made me a great player. **"**

Popovich was persuaded by Tony's promise. Jason Kidd did not become a member of the San Antonio Spurs. The team stuck with Tony at point guard, but he was under great pressure to make good on his word.

During the 2003–04 season, Tony improved noticeably. He finished the year ranked 16th in the NBA in assists while averaging 14.7 points and 3.2 rebounds per game in 75 contests. Also during the course of the regular season, he set single-game bests for assists (14 against the Los Angeles Clippers on December 23) and

CROSS-CURRENTS

Tony Parker is the latest in a long line of standout San Antonio Spurs guards. Go to page 53 to read about a few others. ▶▶

Spurs coach Gregg Popovich gives instructions to his point guard during a 2004 game. Convinced that Tony could become one of the league's premier point guards, Popovich drove his young player hard. While the coach's constant criticism was sometimes difficult to swallow, Tony has credited Popovich for making him a much better player.

steals (six against the Seattle SuperSonics on March 3). And in the 2004 playoffs Tony Parker really shone, averaging 18.4 points, 7.0 assists, 2.1 rebounds and 1.3 steals in 10 postseason contests. The Spurs were eliminated by the L.A. Lakers in the second round of the playoffs and thus failed in their quest to repeat as league champions, but Tony had kept his promise to become a better, more consistent player.

⟫ SWEETER THE SECOND TIME AROUND ⟪

Tony knew his work was far from over. Though he had once felt unfairly criticized by his coach, he realized now that he needed Popovich to push him if he were ever to reach his full potential. The disappointment of failing to return to the 2004 NBA Finals had toughened his skin and increased his drive. There would always, it seemed, be questions regarding Coach Popovich's criticism, but as Tony told Jack Ramsay, former basketball coach and author of *Dr. Jack's Leadership Lessons Learned from a Lifetime in Basketball*:

❝I know that [Coach Popovich] is only trying to get me to do what's best for the team. He's kind of like a father to me. I can take that. ❞

Not only did Tony survive Popovich's harsh critiques, he thrived under his coach's constant scrutiny. The 2004–05 season brought many career highs, including 16.6 points per game, 6.1 assists per contest, and a 48 percent success rate in shooting during the regular season. His shooting percentage was third among all point guards in the NBA, and he was 13th in the league in assists.

His play continued to improve in the 2005 playoffs, when Tony averaged 17.2 points and 4.3 assists, while scoring 10 or more points in all but one of San Antonio's 23 postseason games. The Spurs won the Western Conference and took on the defending champion Detroit Pistons in the NBA Finals. It was a hard-fought, seven-game series between the two ball clubs, but in the end Tony and the Spurs were able to knock off the Pistons and claim the NBA title for the second time in three seasons.

While it was Tony's teammate Tim Duncan who brought home NBA Finals MVP honors, there was little doubt this time around that the young point guard deserved praise for his contributions. As Coach Popovich told author John Hareas after the season ended:

Tony Parker drives past Orlando Magic guard Steve Francis for a layup, December 22, 2004. Tony scored 18 points in the game, but the Magic came out on top, 93–87. Still, San Antonio's record at this point in the season stood at an impressive 20–6, and Tony Parker was a large part of the reason for the Spurs' success.

Tony Parker splits Los Angeles Clippers defenders Chris Kaman (left) and Quinton Ross for a layup, January 19, 2005. Behind Tony's game-high 25 points and seven assists, the Spurs eked out an 80–79 victory to raise their record to 32–9. After notching 59 wins during the 2004–05 regular season, San Antonio would go on to win another title.

> **❝I'm 10,000 times more comfortable with the ball in [Tony's] hands late than I was a couple of years ago. . . . He understands situations much better and sees people much better on the court. No matter what play we call, he reads things and sees other things on the court that might not be there with the play we called, which he wouldn't have seen a couple of years ago.❞**

➤ TAKING IT TO THE NEXT LEVEL ➤

Not everyone was 100 percent satisfied with how Tony Parker played during the 2004–05 season. His chief critic? None other than Tony Parker himself, who told Hareas:

> **❝I think I'm coming a long way since my rookie year. I've established myself as a starting point guard, and now getting closer and closer to the All-Star Game and feeling close to the best point guard in the league. I believe in myself I am one of the best point guards and I can compete against the best on any given night. But I still think I've got a lot of improvement to do in my game. My outside shot can be a lot better, my three-point shot can be more consistent, and my free throws, obviously, I need to improve. And leadership-wise, I still can improve, and the more I'm going to know our guys, and the more we're going to play the big games, I'm going to establish myself as a real point guard, to be the 'Little General' out there.❞**

Bold words, to be sure, but Tony was able to make good on them. Tony started off the 2005–06 season by scoring at least 20 points in seven of San Antonio's first eight games. He scored 30 points against the Dallas Mavericks on December 1 and, a few days later, posted a **double-double** by scoring 14 points and dishing out 11 assists versus the Miami Heat. He added three more double-doubles before the end of the month and continued to run up big numbers well into the new year.

➢ AN ALL-STAR AT LAST ➢

Tony had said that he was getting closer and closer to the All-Star Game. His play during the 2004–05 season was so strong that many, including Parker himself, were surprised that he didn't make the 2005 All-Star team. After his phenomenal play during the first half of the 2005–06 season, however, Tony's status in the league could no longer be denied. He finally earned the honor for the first time in his career and became a member of the 2006 West All-Star team. The ninth Spurs player to be named to an NBA All-Star team, Tony represented the Western Conference well, scoring eight points and adding four assists in 20 minutes. He recalled the experience fondly in comments made on his Web site:

> **“I was very happy to be on the court, it was a lot of emotions. It took me a few minutes to realize everything that was happening. It is incredible to be on the court with such players. I will never forget this evening. I was also lucky to have [former Spurs teammate] Avery Johnson as a coach for the West All Star team. After a mere seven minutes he sent me in the line of duty and it was a great moment.”**

Tony finished the season as strongly has he had started, becoming the first point guard in Spurs history to lead the team in scoring. He had averaged 18.9 points per game, along with 5.8 assists, 3.3 rebounds, and 1.04 steals per contest. His shooting inconsistency was now a thing of the past, as he had the third-highest **field goal** percentage in the NBA, becoming the first point guard to finish that high in almost 30 years. He scored at least 20 points in 30 games and led San Antonio in assists on 50 different occasions in 2005–06. Tony also played incredible basketball in the 2006 postseason, averaging 21.1 points, 3.8 assists, and 3.6 rebounds.

As a team, the Spurs had a stellar season in 2005–06, finishing with a 63–19 mark, which broke the franchise record for regular-season victories. They also qualified for the playoffs for the ninth consecutive season. The Spurs took the opening round of the 2006 playoffs from the Sacramento Kings, four games to two, but they were eliminated in a heartbreaking seven-game series in the second round by Dallas and thus were unable to defend their NBA Championship.

In 2006, in his fifth NBA season, Tony Parker was selected for his first All-Star team. Joining Tony in the front row of this West All-Stars team photo are Steve Nash and Ray Allen. In the back row are (left to right): Shawn Marion, Elton Brand, Kevin Garnett, Dirk Nowitzki, Yao Ming, Pau Gasol, Tim Duncan, Tracy McGrady, and Kobe Bryant.

In his brief career, Tony Parker had faced his shortcomings and he had overcome them. He had enjoyed both team success and personal honors, yet never at the same time. A two-time NBA champion who could now add "NBA All-Star" to his résumé, Tony looked forward to the 2006–07 campaign, hopeful that he would be able to unify personal glory and team achievement in one season.

Tony Parker has come into his own as an NBA star. And, with a popular French-language hip-hop album to his credit— as well as his highly publicized marriage to an American actress—Tony has become something of a celebrity off the basketball court as well.

5

Champion,
On and Off Court

THE 2006–07 SEASON KICKED OFF WITH A BANG for Tony. He scored at least 19 points in each of his first six games. He scored 10 or more points in 15 of the 16 games the Spurs played in the month of November, helping to lead the team to victories in 11 of those contests.

December 8 brought a career-best 15 assists in a victory over the Los Angeles Clippers. He scored 20 or more points nine times during December. Tony was off to the best start of his career. The Spurs were hot as well, losing just three games for the entire month.

Both Tony and the Spurs continued to perform well for the remainder of the 2006–07 campaign. San Antonio finished the regular season with a 58–24 record, good for second place in the Southwest Division and a trip to the playoffs. Tony earned his second consecutive trip to the All-Star Game and finished the season averaging 18.6 points, 5.5 assists, 3.2 rebounds, and 1.06 steals in 77 games. He scored 10 or more points in 68 of his 77 games and was ranked among the NBA's best guards in scoring, assists, and field-goal percentage.

Tony and the Spurs blazed their way through the 2007 playoffs. In the first round, they beat the Denver Nuggets in five games. Next, they eliminated Phoenix in a hard-fought six-game series. San Antonio then won the Western Conference crown by rolling over the Utah Jazz, four games to one, to reach the NBA Finals. The Eastern Conference champion Cleveland Cavaliers, led by LeBron James, were expected to present difficulties for Tony and the Spurs. The Spurs swept Cleveland, however. Tony led the way and was named Finals MVP for his efforts. Finally, he had played through a season that perfectly blended team and personal achievement.

Tony Parker dives to save the ball as Sacramento Kings Mike Bibby (#10) and Justin Williams (#30) look on, April 11, 2007. The Spurs won the game, 109–100, to notch their 57th win of the season. They finished with a regular-season record of 58–24 and rolled to another NBA Championship.

⇒ TONY TIES THE KNOT ⇐

Basketball success was not Tony's only high point in 2007. It was also a banner year for him on the personal front: after the end of the season, he married his longtime girlfriend, actress Eva Longoria. The couple, who had been dating since 2004, was wed on July 7 in France. The ceremony took place at a 17th-century chateau several miles southeast of Paris. More than 200 guests came from around Europe and the United States, including Longoria's *Desperate Housewives* co-stars Teri Hatcher, Nicollette Sheridan, and Felicity Huffman, *American Idol* host Ryan Seacrest, actress Jessica Alba, singer Sheryl Crow, and NBA player Boris Diaw of the Phoenix Suns, a longtime friend of the Spurs point guard.

CROSS-CURRENTS

Read "Eva Longoria Parker" if you would like to learn more about the life and career of Tony Parker's wife. Go to page 54. ▶▶

The wedding received a ton of attention and media coverage—even more, it seemed, than the NBA Finals had. According to a report in *US Magazine*, the date was chosen because Tony is privately a superstitious person, and he believed that the date of "07-07-07" would be lucky. The nuptials were lavish, with a ceremony featuring newly planted gardens, more than 4,000 candles, a fireworks display, and a cake rumored to have cost $11,000. All told, the cost of the ceremony reportedly ran more than half a million dollars, but for Tony and Eva, this was not too much to pay to make their wedding day unforgettable. As the new Mrs. Tony Parker told *Parade* magazine:

> **"Every time I think of my wedding, I just smile. . . . It's funny, because it's so cliché for women to say, 'My wedding was the happiest day of my life.' But I find myself saying that and thinking, 'Yes, my wedding was the happiest day of my life so far.'"**

The attention of the press only increased after the wedding between the Hollywood star and the NBA star. With millions watching her in *Desperate Housewives* on television every week, Eva Longoria was probably more famous than Tony, and the tabloids covered every move they made, often with pictures as well as stories. Holding hands, sunning themselves, even Tony losing his bathing trunks as

The Hollywood star and the hardwood star: Eva Longoria and Tony Parker at the 2007 ALMA Awards, Pasadena, California, June 1, 2007. Sponsored by the National Council of La Raza—the largest Hispanic civil rights and advocacy organization in the United States—the ALMA Awards honor the work of Latinos in film, television, and music. Longoria hosted the 2007 awards ceremony.

he dove into the water from a yacht . . . everything was captured and splashed over the Internet and cable TV. Hurtful rumors flourished, too, as scandal seekers looked for signs of problems in the celebrity marriage. Just months after the wedding a French fashion model claimed to be having an affair with Tony. Spokesmen for the couple were swift to deny the charge and proclaim that all was well in the Parker-Longoria household.

⟫ LIFE OUTSIDE OF BASKETBALL ⟪

With his celebrity growing on and off the court, Tony branched out into other projects during 2007. He recorded an album of French-language hip-hop songs and saw one of the singles, a song called "Balance-toi," go to number one on the charts in his home country, selling more than 10,000 copies during its first week of release. Tony is passionate about music, as he writes on his homepage:

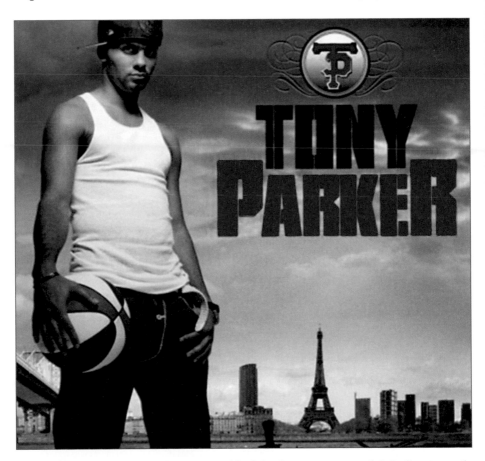

The album cover of Tony's self-titled 2007 CD, which featured 11 hip-hop tracks. The single "Balance Toi," which reached number one on the French charts, is about the nightclub scene and contained references to Tony's longtime girlfriend and soon-to-be wife, Eva Longoria. Tony, a lifelong fan of rap music, lists Jay-Z, Eminem, and 50 Cent among his favorite artists.

"It is a good breath of air. With the pressure in basketball, I can disconnect everything and think of something else by locking myself in the studio. This album is a childhood dream that comes to life. I have [had] a true passion for my music since I was a kid. Now I can show to everyone that I have worked hard. . . . Behind this album you have months of work.**"**

Using his fame to help others allows Tony to give back some of his good fortune. He currently holds the position of first ambassador for the Make-A-Wish Foundation in France. In addition, according to his biography at NBA.com, Tony donates a block of 20 tickets to every Spurs home game to underprivileged youth. Furthermore, he has long been involved with the Basketball Without Borders project, the NBA's international basketball and community-outreach program. Working with this program, Tony has visited other countries, talking and playing with kids around the world as a coach and mentor.

CROSS-CURRENTS

To learn more about a charitable organization for which Tony serves as a high-profile ambassador, read "The Make-A-Wish Foundation." Go to page 55. ▶▶

Although Tony's travels and community projects keep him busy when he's not on the court, he still has time for fun and for projects close to his heart. He threw his celebrity and his powers of persuasion behind the unsuccessful attempt to bring the 2012 Summer Olympic Games to Paris and was as disappointed as any Frenchman when the Olympics were awarded to London instead. He is also an avid and longtime fan of video games, which makes even more noteworthy the fact that 2007 marked the third straight year in which he appeared on the cover of the EA Sports *NBA Live* video game in his home country.

All in all, 2007 was a busy off-season for Tony Parker. But soon the honeymoon was over. Once again, it was time for Tony to step back onto the **hardwood** and do his thing.

⟫ 2007–08: FACING SETBACKS, COMING BACK ⟪

As the 2007–08 season started, Tony picked up where right where he had left off, determined to make his seventh season in the NBA his best yet. In his first 39 games of the year, thanks in part to several games in which he scored around the 30-point mark, Tony averaged 19.2 points, 6.1 assists, and 3.0 rebounds per game.

NBA star Tony Parker talks to a group of kids visiting the Humane Society of Bexar County, San Antonio, Texas, January 9, 2008. Tony donates time and money to a variety of charitable causes and organizations. Among his favorites is the Make-A-Wish Foundation.

But his glowing statistics didn't tell the whole story. Tony had been playing much of the first half of the season with both a bone spur in his left foot and an inflamed left ankle. As the numbers showed, he was not letting the injuries slow him down. His foot was not getting better, however, and on January 30 the Spurs put Tony on the inactive list to allow him time to heal. Being the headstrong competitor that he is, Tony had trouble accepting that anything should keep him off the court. However, he eventually came to see his coach's point that his long-term well-being was more important than playing through the pain.

Seven-foot center Chris Kaman has him covered, so Tony Parker attempts a no-look, behind-the-back pass to his Spurs teammate Tim Duncan, March 26, 2008. Injuries had forced Tony to sit out much of February, but he played well upon returning to the San Antonio lineup.

Tony came back from his injury within a month, helping San Antonio secure a spot in the 2008 playoffs. Both Tony and the Spurs played convincingly against their first-round opponents, the Phoenix Suns, taking the first three games and winning the series four games to one. Tony averaged over 29 points per game in that series.

New Orleans was a formidable second-round foe, jumping off to a 2–0 series lead. The Spurs then came roaring back to tie the series at two apiece. The teams then traded wins, and they traveled back to New Orleans for the decisive seventh game. Despite allowing a 17-point lead to dwindle to 3 points in the fourth quarter, the

"When you play for team like the San Antonio Spurs," Tony Parker said after the 2007–08 season, "there is a lot of pressure. The only goal is to win the title." Spurs fans know that the talented and hardworking point guard from France will do his part to bring another NBA Championship to their city.

Spurs held on and prevailed, 91–82. Fueled by the momentum of this exciting semifinal series, Tony Parker and his teammates were confident as they headed into the Western Conference Finals against the Los Angeles Lakers.

In Game 1, played at the Staples Center in Los Angeles on May 21, Tony turned in a solid performance. He scored 18 points, dished six assists, and grabbed 10 rebounds. Led by Kobe Bryant's 27 points, however, the Lakers won, 89–85. Two days later, the Spurs came out flat and received a 101–71 beating. The series resumed in San Antonio on May 25. Inspired by their fans, the Spurs took Game 3 by a score of 103–84. Tony chipped in with 20 points.

But hopes for another San Antonio comeback were dashed in Game 4. Despite Tony's 23 points and nine assists, Los Angeles dealt the hometown Spurs a bitter 93–91 defeat and took a three-games-to-one series lead. The Spurs' season came to an end on May 29 at the Staples Center. Tony's 23 points weren't enough to prevent a 100–92 Game 5 victory for Los Angeles.

⇒ BANKING ON A ROSY FUTURE ⇐

Despite his team's 2008 playoff setback, no one could deny that Tony Parker had come into his own. Still young, he had already accomplished many things in the NBA. He was one of just five guards to have made at least two All-Star Game appearances by the age of 25, and he was second in playoff scoring and third in playoff assists among players age 25 or younger. Given his immense physical ability, his tremendous work ethic, and his dedication to improving both his team and his community, it is a safe bet that Tony Parker will be a basketball star and a role model for years to come.

The San Antonio Spurs

Thanks largely to Tony Parker's contributions, the San Antonio Spurs won their fourth NBA Championship in 2007. Established in 1967, the franchise now known as the Spurs started as the Dallas Chaparrals of the American Basketball Association (ABA). The Chaparrals went 46–32 and made the **playoffs** during their first season. Afterward, however, struggles on the court and attendance woes would ultimately force major changes. In 1973, the team was sold. The new owners moved the team to San Antonio and renamed it the Spurs.

When the ABA folded following the 1975–76 season, the Spurs became one of four teams absorbed into the National Basketball Association (NBA). The Spurs won their first NBA game, downing the Philadelphia 76ers, 121–118, on October 22, 1976. San Antonio made the NBA playoffs that year but was eliminated in the first round. Not making it past the first round would emerge as a trend that would repeat itself often as years passed.

Many coaches and players came and went between the 1976–77 season and San Antonio's first NBA Championship in 1999, when David Robinson and Tim Duncan led the Spurs to victory against the New York Knicks in five games. San Antonio went on to win titles in 2003, 2005, and 2007.

(Go back to page 6.) ◀◀

European Player of the Year Award

Among Tony's accomplishments in 2007 was receiving the European Player of the Year award. The award is handed out by *La Gazzetta dello Sport*, an Italian newspaper that covers sports stories throughout the continent. *La Gazzetta dello Sport* was first published in 1896 and covered the first modern Olympic Games, which were held that year in Athens, Greece. These days, it sells more than 40,000 copies per day and is read by nearly 3 million people worldwide.

The newspaper has bestowed its European Player of the Year award since 1979, making Tony Parker the 29th recipient of the honor. Former Ukrainian basketball star Vladimir Tkachenko was the first. Other NBA players to have been named European Player of the Year include Lithuania's Arvydas Sabonis of the Portland Trail Blazers and Toni Kukoc, who came to the Milwaukee Bucks from Croatia. Dallas Maverick Dirk Nowitzki from Germany had won the honor five years running before finishing second to Parker for 2007, with third place for that year going to Russian Andrei Kirilenko of the Utah Jazz. The award recipient is chosen annually by a panel of 100 sportswriters, athletes, and coaches from more than two dozen countries.

(Go back to page 9.)

Facts About France

Although he was born in Bruges, Belgium, Tony Parker considers France his home. France is the largest nation in Western Europe, covering about 211,150 square miles (547,030 sq km). It also controls some overseas territories, such as French Guiana in South America and the islands of Guadeloupe, Martinique, and Réunion. The population of France is approximately 60 million.

A Long National History

While some people can trace their roots in France to the fifth century, it was the Treaty of Verdun in A.D. 843 that divided the ruler Charlemagne's large kingdom into three parts. One of these became the nation known today as France, so most people mark 843 as the year of France's birth as a nation. For centuries, France was the strongest European kingdom, although it often battled with England, Spain, and Germany for its position. In 1778, the French government agreed to send weapons, money, and soldiers to help the Americans win their freedom from Great Britain. Under the rule of Napoleon (1799–1815), France briefly conquered most of Europe. However, an alliance of European countries eventually defeated Napoleon and checked France's expansion.

During the 20th century, France was the site of many important battles in both World War I and World War II. Although the French emerged on the winning side in both conflicts, the wars left France weakened as a world power. After the Second World War ended, France played an important role in creating agreements for cooperation among European states. These agreements eventually led to the formation of the European Union, a political and economic organization of European countries.

Modern-day France

Today, France is a democratic republic. Its government is run by a president and a bicameral Parliament, which is a two-house system similar to the U.S. Congress. The current president of France, Nicolas Sarkozy, was elected in May 2007. France is also a key member of the European Union.

The capital of France is Paris, which is also the largest city in the country and one of the most popular tourist destinations in the world today. The French people are known for their fine style and wonderful food. Paintings by French artists Pierre-Auguste Renoir, Claude Monet, and Paul Cezanne are treasured by museumgoers throughout the world. Each year a film festival in the city of Cannes and fashion shows in Paris attract the attention of the beautiful and the talented—and those who like to watch them.

(Go back to page 11.)

The Eiffel Tower, in Paris, France, is one of the world's most recognizable landmarks. The iron structure, which rises more than 1,000 feet (324 meters), was the tallest building in the world when completed in 1889. It was unveiled that year to commemorate the hundredth anniversary of the French Revolution.

Other European NBA Players

Tony Parker may be able to claim a lot of firsts among European basketball players. But he was not the first European player to make it to the NBA, and he wasn't the first great one. One of the pioneers of the European movement in American basketball was German-born Detlef Schrempf, who was drafted by the Dallas Mavericks in 1985. Schrempf played until 2001, appearing in over 1,100 games and scoring more than 15,000 points during his career. In addition, he was a three-time NBA All-Star and a two-time winner of the NBA Sixth Man of the Year Award.

Dallas Mavericks big man Dirk Nowitzki is one of the best basketball players to come out of Europe. The seven-footer, born in Germany in 1978, was drafted by the NBA's Milwaukee Bucks in 1998. He was immediately traded to the Mavericks, where he has played his entire career. Nowitzki, an excellent shooter and rebounder, was named the NBA's MVP in 2007.

Joining Tony Parker and Schrempf in a long list of talented European players is former Los Angeles Lakers and Sacramento Kings star Vlade Divac of Serbia. Divac is one of just three players in NBA history to amass 13,000 points, 9,000 rebounds, 3,000 assists, and 1,500 blocked shots during his career. Peja Stojakovic, also from Serbia, is a three-time NBA All-Star and a two-time winner of the annual NBA All-Star Three Point competition. Germany's Dirk Nowitzki of the Dallas Mavericks is a seven-time All-Star and was named the 2007 NBA Most Valuable Player. They are just a few of the many talented European basketball players to have made their mark on the NBA.

(Go back to page 14.)

The Man Called Pop

Perhaps no other figure was more influential in Tony Parker's basketball career than his coach with the Spurs, Gregg Popovich. "Coach Pop" has long been a mentor to Tony. He was born in 1949 in East Chicago, Indiana. Like Tony Parker, Popovich traces his roots back to Europe. His father was Serbian and his mother was from Croatia.

Popovich attended and played basketball for the Air Force Academy, leading the team in scoring during his senior season. He was also captain of the Armed Forces squad that won the **Amateur Athletic Union** (AAU) championship in 1972. In 1973, he returned to the Academy to begin his coaching career as an assistant with his old team, the Falcons. After six years, Popovich left the Academy and was named head coach for Pomona-Pitzer in Claremont, California. While there, he led the school to its first conference title in nearly seven decades and a berth in the 1985–86 Division III Tournament.

In 1988, Popovich joined the Spurs for the first time, as an assistant on the staff of head coach Larry Brown. He and Brown became friends and won two Midwest Division titles before both coaches, along with the rest of the San Antonio coaching staff, were fired in 1992. Popovich spent the next two seasons with the Golden State Warriors before rejoining the Spurs as vice president of basketball operations and general manager in 1994. Two seasons later, he fired Bob Hill as head coach and took over as the team's interim coach.

Popovich struggled early on, with a 17–47 record during the 1996–97 season. Those early difficulties did not last. After that season, the Spurs won the first pick in the NBA draft and selected Tim Duncan out of Wake Forest University. Duncan had an immediate impact, and the team improved to 56–26 in 1997–98. In 1999 Coach Pop guided the Spurs to their first NBA Championship.

Popovich showed that his draft judgment was not a fluke when he picked Tony Parker in 2001. With Popovich as head coach, the Spurs won NBA titles in 2003, 2005, and 2007. Popovich is just the fifth NBA coach to win four championships in his career, and he is the winningest coach in Spurs history.

(Go back to page 17.) ◀◀

International Sports Stars

Tony Parker is a hero to sports fans in his native France, but he is not the only athlete to have an impact on his home country while playing for an American professional team. Fellow NBA star Yao Ming of the Houston Rockets has been an icon in his native China for many years. A former NBA Rookie of the Year and six-time NBA All-Star, Yao holds the record for most votes received in All-Star Game **balloting**. Because of him, broadcasts of Rockets games in China draw hundreds of millions of viewers.

A poster for the 2004 film The Year of the Yao. *The documentary chronicled basketball star Yao Ming's rookie season in the NBA, showing how he fared on the court, how he adapted to life in the United States, and how basketball fans embraced the big man from China. Yao is one of the most famous international sports icons.*

Like Tony Parker and Yao Ming, Ichiro Suzuki and David Beckham have become sports stars worldwide. Ichiro, an outfielder for the Seattle Mariners, holds the Major League record for most hits in a season. Like Yao, Ichiro dominates All-Star voting. With the help of fans in Japan, Ichiro became the first rookie to lead the American League in All-Star voting. Furthermore, Japanese news programs broadcast each of his at-bats during a game. Beckham is a professional soccer player who has twice won the FIFA Player of the Year Award. His name is known worldwide, and, whether he likes it or not, his wife, former Spice Girl Victoria Beckham, guarantees his place in the spotlight off the field. Beckham has become one of the most highly sought after and well paid spokespeople in the world.

(Go back to page 27.) ◀◀

Other Great Spurs Guards

When Tony Parker became the first San Antonio Spurs point guard to lead the team in scoring, it was no small feat. During the team's history, many great players had played at the guard position, among them James Silas, Johnny Moore , and Avery Johnson.

Born in Tallulah, Louisiana, in 1949, James Silas was originally drafted by the NBA's Houston Rockets but was released before playing a single game. The Dallas Chaparrals, the team that would become the San Antonio Spurs, signed Silas to a contract. Silas had a great year and was named 1972–73 ABA Rookie of the Year. Next year, the team became the Spurs, and Silas became famous for last-second, game winning shots, earning the nickname "Captain Late." When Silas retired in 1982, he was San Antonio's all-time leader in games played, points scored, and steals. His number 13 jersey was the first retired by the Spurs.

Sadly, Johnny Moore's career was cut short by a rare illness known as desert fever, but the point guard from Altoona, Pennsylvania, took full advantage of every opportunity he had. Moore played in 520 NBA games between 1980 and 1990 and, at the end of his career, was the Spurs' all-time leader with 3,685 assists. He also was second in team history with 1,017 steals and set a franchise single-game playoff record with 20 assists in a 1983 game against the Denver Nuggets. Moore's number, 00, was retired by the team at the end of his career. In 2003, he was inducted into the San Antonio Sports Hall of Fame.

Avery Johnson was a key player on the 1999 team that won the Spurs' first NBA Championship. Following a solid college basketball career, Johnson signed a free-agent contract with the Seattle SuperSonics in 1988. "The Little General," as he was known, played 16 seasons for six different teams, but spent most of his NBA career with the Spurs, who retired his number 6 on December 22, 2007. During his career, Johnson amassed 5,846 assists, 8,817 points, and 1,007 steals. When his playing days ended, Johnson began a career in coaching. In 2006 he was named NBA Coach of the Year for his success as the head coach of the Dallas Mavericks. (Go back to page 28.) ◀◀

Avery Johnson, a 5'11" point guard nicknamed "the Little General," helped lead the 1998–99 San Antonio Spurs to the first NBA Championship in franchise history. Johnson clinched the title by hitting a baseline jumper late in the decisive Game 5.

Eva Longoria Parker

Tony Parker's wife, Eva Longoria Parker, was born on March 15, 1975, in Corpus Christi, Texas. She was the youngest child of Enrique and Ella Longoria and has three sisters, Liza, Emily, and Esmeralda. Eva went to college at Texas A&M University-Kingsville, graduating from there with a Bachelor of Science degree in Kinesiology. While still in school, she was named Miss Corpus Christi USA of 1998. Following her graduation, she won a talent competition that landed her an agent and a trip to Los Angeles. That would mark the beginning of her acting career.

Following a series of guest spots, Eva's first major acting gig came when she landed the role of Isabella Brana Williams on the daytime drama *The Young and the Restless*. She remained on the show until 2003 and won an American Latino Media Arts (ALMA) Award in 2002 for her performance. In 2004, she appeared in her most famous role to date as Gabrielle Solis in the new ABC show *Desperate Housewives*. The show was a great hit, and her performance earned Eva a 2006 Golden Globe nomination and Hollywood star status. She has also appeared in several motion pictures, including *The Sentinel*, *The Heartbreak Kid*, and *Over Her Dead Body*.

Tony Parker is Eva's second husband—she was married to actor Tyler Christopher from January 2002 to January 2004.

(Go back to page 39.)

Actress Eva Longoria, who married Tony Parker in July 2007, graces the cover of the April 7–9, 2006, edition of USA Weekend. *Longoria gained fame for her role in the ABC television series* Desperate Housewives. *She has also appeared in several motion pictures.*

The Make-A-Wish Foundation

Tony Parker works enthusiastically with the Make-A-Wish Foundation in France. The Make-A-Wish Foundation is a nonprofit organization founded in 1980. Its purpose is to provide children who have life-threatening medical conditions with an opportunity to have their wishes granted, allowing them to participate in events that they've always dreamed of. The first wish granted by what would eventually become the Make-A-Wish Foundation was in Phoenix, Arizona, where a young boy with leukemia was given the opportunity to be a police officer for a day. Since then, the organization has helped more than 160,000 children worldwide.

The Make-A-Wish Foundation opened its international branch in 1993 and now serves children and families in 28 countries located on five continents. Joining Tony as an ambassador for Make-A-Wish France are soccer star Jean-Alain Boumsong, auto racing's Henri Pescarolo, and fashion designer Jean Doucet. Together, the quartet helped Make-A-Wish France raise more than 200,000 Euros in 2007. That's nearly $300,000 in U.S. dollars. According to the official Make-A-Wish France Web site, much of the credit

Seven-year-old Brianna Duarte unveils a poster for the Make-A-Wish Foundation, Los Angeles, November 1, 2006. The photo on the poster shows Brianna realizing her dream to become "princess for a day." The Make-A-Wish Foundation, one of Tony Parker's favorite charities, helps children with life-threatening medical conditions.

belonged to Tony, who spearheaded an effort to bring in donations from a wide variety of sports stars and entertainment icons.

(Go back to page 42.) ◀◀

1982 William Anthony Parker is born on May 17 in Bruges, Belgium.

1996 After attending Chicago Bulls practice and meeting Michael Jordan while on vacation in Illinois, Tony dedicates himself to basketball.

1997 Tony is named Most Valuable Player (MVP) of the Salbris Junior Tournament.

1999 Tony signs with Paris Basket Racing, thus beginning his professional basketball career.

2000 Tony is invited to participate in the Nike Hoops Summit, where he impresses collegiate and pro scouts with a strong performance.

2001 Tony decides not to go to college and enters the NBA draft; he is selected 28th overall by the San Antonio Spurs. He makes his NBA debut on October 30.

2003 His sophomore season ends in championship fashion, as Tony and the Spurs beat the New Jersey Nets in the NBA Finals.

2005 Tony earns his second NBA Championship ring as the Spurs beat the Detroit Pistons in the Finals.

2006 Tony earns NBA All-Star honors for the first time in his career and leads the Spurs in scoring for the 2005–06 season.

2007 Tony leads the Spurs to another NBA Championship, earning Finals MVP honors in the process. Later in the year, he marries actress Eva Longoria.

2008 Tony overcomes a season-threatening bone spur in his left foot to help the Spurs capture a playoff berth for the 11th consecutive season.

AWARDS AND CHAMPIONSHIPS

1996 Salbris Junior Tournament MVP

2000 European Junior League Champion
European Junior League MVP

2001 French Championship Rookie of the Year

2002 NBA All-Rookie First Team Selection

2003 NBA Champion (with Spurs)

2005 NBA Champion (with Spurs)
Bronze Medal (European Championship)

2006 NBA All-Star

2007 NBA All-Star, NBA Champion (with Spurs)
NBA Finals MVP
European Player of the Year

CAREER HIGHS

Points—41 @ Phoenix, 04/25/08

Field Goals Made—15 @ Golden State, 04/10/05

Field Goals Attempted—31 @ Phoenix, 03/09/05

Three-Point Field Goals Made—4 (6 times)

Three-Point Field Goals Attempted—8 (2 times)

Free Throws Made—14 vs. Boston, 03/17/07

Free Throws Attempted—14 (3 times)

Offensive Rebounds—3 (5 times)

Defensive Rebounds—9 (2 times)

Total Rebounds—10 (times)

Assists—15 vs. L.A. Clippers, 12/08/06

Steals—6 vs. Seattle, 03/03/04

Minutes Played—53 @ L.A. Clippers, 04/09/05

REGULAR SEASON STATISTICS

Year	Team	G	GS	MPG	FG%	3P%	FT%	OFF	DEF	RPG	APG	SPG	BPG	TO	PF	PPG
01-02	Spurs	77	72	29.4	0.419	0.323	0.675	0.4	2.1	2.6	4.3	1.2	0.1	1.96	2.20	9.2
02-03	Spurs	82	82	33.8	0.464	0.337	0.755	0.4	2.2	2.6	5.3	0.9	0.1	2.41	2.10	15.5
03-04	Spurs	75	75	34.4	0.447	0.312	0.702	0.6	2.6	3.2	5.5	0.8	0.1	2.39	2.00	14.7
04-05	Spurs	80	80	34.2	0.482	0.276	0.650	0.6	3.1	3.7	6.1	1.2	0.1	2.69	2.10	16.6
05-06	Spurs	80	80	33.9	0.548	0.306	0.707	0.5	2.8	3.3	5.8	1.0	0.1	3.11	2.00	18.9
06-07	Spurs	77	77	32.5	0.520	0.395	0.783	0.4	2.8	3.2	5.5	1.1	0.1	2.48	1.80	18.6
07-08	Spurs	69	68	33.5	0.494	0.258	0.715	0.54	2.8	3.2	6.0	0.8	0.1	2.38	1.13	18.8
Career	—	540	534	33.1	0.487	0.314	0.716	0.5	2.6	3.1	5.5	1.0	0.0	2.49	1.90	16.0

PLAYOFF STATISTICS

Year	Team	G	GS	MPG	FG%	3P%	FT%	OFF	DEF	RPG	APG	SPG	BPG	TO	PF	PPG
01-02	Spurs	10	10	34.1	0.456	0.370	0.750	0.5	2.4	2.9	4.0	0.9	0.1	2.20	2.20	15.5
02-03	Spurs	24	24	33.9	0.403	0.268	0.713	0.3	2.4	2.8	3.5	0.9	0.1	1.96	2.10	14.7
03-04	Spurs	10	10	38.6	0.429	0.395	0.657	0.5	1.6	2.1	7.0	1.3	0.1	3.10	1.50	18.4
04-05	Spurs	23	23	37.3	0.454	0.188	0.632	0.6	2.3	2.9	4.3	0.7	0.1	3.09	3.00	17.2
05-06	Spurs	13	13	36.5	0.460	0.222	0.810	0.6	3.0	3.6	3.8	1.0	0.1	3.08	2.40	21.1
06-07	Spurs	20	20	37.6	0.480	0.333	0.679	0.7	2.7	3.4	5.8	1.1	0.0	3.30	1.70	20.8
07-08	Spurs	17	17	38.5	0.497	0.350	0.753	0.6	3.1	3.7	6.1	0.9	0.1	2.94	2.20	22.4
Career	—	117	117	36.6	0.455	0.299	0.713	0.5	2.5	3.1	4.8	1.0	0.1	2.79	2.20	18.4

Books

Bednar, Chuck. *The San Antonio Spurs*. San Diego: Lucent Books, 2003.

Finkel, Jon. *Greatest Stars of the NBA: Guards Edition*. Los Angeles: Tokyopop, 2007.

Hareas, John. *One Team. One Goal. Mission Accomplished: The 2005 NBA Champion San Antonio Spurs*. Daytona Beach, FL.: EventDay Media, 2005.

LeBoutillier, Nate. *The Story of the San Antonio Spurs*. Mankato, Minn.: Creative Education, 2006.

Ramsay, Jack. *Dr. Jack's Leadership Lessons Learned from a Lifetime in Basketball*. Hoboken, N.J.: John Wiley and Sons, 2004.

Stewart, Mark. *The San Antonio Spurs*. Chicago: Norwood House Press, 2006.

Web Sites

http://www.tp9.net/en/index1.php

Tony Parker's official Web site includes interviews with the Spurs point guard, news, photos, multimedia features, biographical information, and more.

http://www.nba.com/playerfile/tony_parker

Parker's biography at NBA.com, the official Web site of the National Basketball Association. Also includes links to video highlights, career statistics, and background info.

http://www.nba.com/spurs/

The official homepage of Tony Parker's team, the San Antonio Spurs. It includes team news, statistics, the current season's schedule, and much more.

http://www.basketball-reference.com/

Basketball-Reference.com, a comprehensive collection of basketball statistics and player information.

http://espn.go.com/

The Internet home of the ESPN television network contains in-depth coverage of a variety of sports, including NBA basketball, as well as detailed information about various athletes and sports teams.

Publisher's note:

The Web sites mentioned in this book were active at the time of publication. The publisher is not responsible for Web sites that have changed their addresses or discontinued operation since the date of publication. The publisher will review and update the Web site addresses each time the book is reprinted.

Amateur Athletic Union (AAU)—an organization that promotes non-professional sporting events in the United States, often through sports programs throughout the nation and the formation of teams in competitive play, including championship events.

assist—the basketball statistic that records how many times one player passes the ball to another right before the second player scores a basket.

balloting—voting.

court—the term used to describe the 94-foot by 50-foot playing surface on which professional basketball games are played.

double-double—an individual performance in which a player has double-digit numbers in two of the following categories: points, rebounds, assists, steals, or blocked shots.

draft—in sports, the annual process by which teams select new players from the college or amateur ranks, with teams that performed poorly during the past season picking before those with good records.

executing—putting into action (as a plan).

field goal—a successful shot that is worth two or three points, depending on how far from the basket the shooter was.

franchise—a team in a professional sports league.

hardwood—another name for a basketball court, so named because of the playing surface traditionally used.

MVP—abbreviation for Most Valuable Player, an award given to a player for exceptional performance during a season, game, or playoff series.

playoffs—series of games played following the regular season in which the best teams compete against each other in order to determine a league champion.

point guard—the player on a basketball team who is usually in charge of running the offense by calling plays and passing the ball to open teammates.

rebound—the act of gaining possession of the basketball following a failed attempted shot, either by a teammate (offensive rebound) or by an opponent (defensive rebound).

rookie—a professional athlete who is playing in his or her first year.

shooting percentage—the ratio of successful baskets made by a player or team to the number of shots attempted.

steal—either the act of legally taking possession of the basketball from an opponent; or, as *steals*, the statistic that records the number of times that this feat has been accomplished.

three-point—referring to a shot that originates from behind a line drawn 23 feet, 9 inches (at its greatest distance) away from the basket. Such a shot is worth three points on the scoreboard instead of the customary two because of the distance.

page 6 "That would be unbelievable . . ." Martin Sumners, "Dreams Do Come True." NBA.com (June 15, 2007). http://www.nba.com/finals2007/news/parker_mvp_070614.html

page 9 "It's great, it's great . . ." InsideHoops.com Newswire, "Tony Parker interview after winning Finals MVP." Inside Hoops.com (June 15, 2007). http://www.insidehoops.com/parker-interview-061507.shtml

page 12 "It is not easy . . ." Quoted in "From INSEP to PSG," TP9.net. http://www.tp9.net/en/viebio3.htm

page 14 "For all basketball players . . ." Quoted in "The American Dream," TP9.net. http://www.tp9.net/en/viebio4.htm

page 14 "He was playing . . ." David DuPree, "The Buford Way: Spurs' Architect Stays in Shadows," USAToday.com (May 21, 2007). http://www.usatoday.com/sports/basketball/nba/spurs/2007-05-21-cover-buford_N.htm

page 17 "There [were] growing pains . . ." Dan Wetzel, "French Connection," Yahoo! Sports (June 14, 2007). http://sports.yahoo.com/nba/news?slug=dw-parker061507&prov=yhoo&type=lgns

page 18 "I never lost my confidence . . ." Johnny Ludden, "Spurs, Parker earn win over Dallas," *San Antonio Express-News*/MySA.com (December 12, 2002). http://www.mysanantonio.com/specials/spurschamps/stories/892594.shtml

page 25 "Parker knew he would . . ." Johnny Ludden, "Spurs start slow, upend Nets on road," *San Antonio Express-News*/MySA.com (June 9, 2003). http://www.mysanantonio.com/specials/spurschamps/stories/1009267.shtml

page 27 "Since his first . . ." Ian Whittell, "French love all things Parker," ESPN.com (October 16, 2006). http://sports.espn.go.com/nba/trainingcamp06/columns/story?id=2617636

page 28 "[It] was a tough time . . ." Wetzel, "French Connection."

page 30 "I know that [Coach Popovich] . . ." Jack Ramsay, *Dr. Jack's Leadership Lessons Learned from a Lifetime in Basketball* (Hoboken, NJ: John Wiley & Sons, 2004), p. 54.

page 33 "I'm 10,000 times more comfortable . . ." John Hareas, *One Team. One Goal. Mission Accomplished: The 2005 NBA Champion San Antonio Spurs* (Daytona Beach, FL: EventDay Media, 2005), p. 26.

page 33 "I think I'm coming . . ." Hareas, *One Team. One Goal. Mission Accomplished: The 2005 NBA Champion San Antonio Spurs*, p. 26.

page 34 "I was very happy . . ." Quoted in "A lot of emotions," TP9.net (February 19, 2006). http://www.tp9.net/en/itw.php?id=114

page 39 "Every time I think of . . ." Jeanne Wolf, *Parade* Magazine (November 25, 2007). http://www.parade.com/articles/editions/2007/edition_11-25-2007/Eva_Longoria

page 42 "It is a good breath . . ." Quoted in "A good breath of air," TP9.net (March 20, 2007). http://www.tp9.net/en/itw.php?id=170

Chuck Bednar is an author and freelance writer currently residing in Ohio. He is the author of five other sports-related books, including *The San Antonio Spurs* (Lucent, 2003). Chuck is currently working as forum administrator for GoTeamsGo.com.

PICTURE CREDITS